MW00989724

Answers to Your Cell Group Questions

Answers to Your Cell Group Questions

RANDALL G. NEIGHBOUR

TOUCH PUBLICATIONS
Houston, Texas, U.S.A.

Published by TOUCH Publications
P.O. Box 19888
Houston, Texas, 77224-9888, U.S.A.
(281) 497-7901 • Fax (281) 497-0904

Cover design by Don Bleyl
Text design by Rick Chandler
Editing by Scott Boren

International Standard Book Number: 1-880828-25-1

TOUCH Publications is the book-publishing division
of TOUCH Outreach Ministries, a resource and
consulting ministry for churches with a vision for
cell-based local church structure.

Find us on the World Wide Web at
http://www.touchusa.org

Table of Contents

Introduction 7

Section 1
Leading the Meeting 9

Section 2
Developing Leaders 25

Section 3
Entering into Community 41

Section 4
Reaching Out 57

Section 5
Expanding the Cell 75

Introduction

Leading a cell group has been, and will always be, the most challenging thing I do. Since the late 1970's, I've been a cell leader and it pushes me to serve others when I'm not motivated and to increase my prayer life for people and problems I can't fix. Cell leadership has forced me to mature in Christ. For this reason I plan to be a cell leader for the rest of my life. I don't aspire to become a senior pastor or missionary. This is too good!

When I see my cell members realize their potential by leading friends to Christ and moving into leadership, I know I've done something important for the kingdom. I also have found that my current cell group is closer to me than my own earthly family. We spend lots of time laughing and joking with each other.

As I travel and speak about cell life and leadership, people ask me to address specific problems that come up in their groups. The details vary, but most of the questions have common themes. While my answers are not perfect, I've been a cell leader long enough to have faced most of the typical problems. In some cases, I could have handled the situation better; therefore much of the advice is based on personal trial and error. Failure is the best teacher, so as you read, know that I'm writing from experience . . . good and bad!

These answers will challenge you to take new steps as a cell leader. If an answer doesn't go far enough or work for your particular situation, do what I do. Drop to your knees and ask God for the answer. He has always been faithful to direct my words and attitudes.

A cell leader once asked me, "What is the most memorable thing that has happened to you in a cell meeting?" There is so much competition between stories that I must share more than one!

My worst cell meeting experience happened when my members shared how I could be a better leader . . . and they were all right. The next would be when a recently released prison inmate visited our group and stood up to put his fist in the face of a cell member. Instead of breaking up the fight, my intern shouted, "Praise God, we've broken through to the conflict stage!"

My funniest cell meeting memory is of an older intern who fell asleep while facilitating the ministry time. We all slipped out of the room and went into the kitchen for a snack. He finally woke up when we could not contain our laughter.

I will always remember the meeting when a new friend gave his heart to Jesus. I asked him if we could hold hands and close our eyes while he prayed the "sinner's prayer." Being so new to Christianity, he asked if this was mandatory. I told him it wasn't but it would keep me from running around the room from excitement!

I'm sure you have a few stories too. One day I hope to learn from your experience. Enjoy what you find here, and when the going gets tough, remember that the tough pray harder than the rest!

Leading the Meeting

Leading the Meeting

uestion: **CELL AGENDAS**

I need some good cell agendas for my weekly meetings, and I don't know what to do. Can you give me some ideas?

nswer: There are lots of creative ways to get people talking and ministering to each other in your next meeting!

1. Listen carefully during your pastor's sermon. Try writing up discussion questions as you sit in the weekly service. First, write down the scripture reference and the title of the sermon, as well as a few notes about the basis of what he's talking about (sometimes sermons have unusual surprise titles!).

Next, write down a closed-ended question to help everyone in the group focus on the verse you are discussing. A closed-ended question is one that usually has only one right answer that is drawn from the scripture passage.

Then, write down a standard question that varies from week to week, but sounds something like "Can anyone illustrate what we're talking about here from your own life?" This gets cell members sharing their past experiences.

Next, write down a ministry question such as "According to this passage, what must you confess tonight or change in your life to live out God's will for your life?"

Last, bring the group to a place where you plan, pray, and discuss your purpose in life, which is to reach people for Jesus and show them how to do the same thing. Pray for lost people, and determine where your "*oikos*" thread is in the group (usually a member with lots of unbelievers you need to meet and get to know).

Finally, you should always select an appropriate icebreaker to open the meeting and get everyone talking.

2. Go to a Christian bookstore and buy a Serendipity Bible for Study Groups by Zondervan. This is an invaluable source of questions for every chapter of the Bible. The only thing you have to remember when using the questions found in this unique tool is that it's really designed for Bible studies. What I like about it is that it has good icebreakers, thought-provoking questions, and it's doctrinally sound. This isn't my first suggestion because if you can tie your cell meeting subject matter to your celebration service, your members will be more likely to become faithful attendees. It also helps members from other churches who visit your cell know that it's a vital part of your church, not a community Bible study for anyone who wants to attend.

3. There are 12 sample cell agendas in the back of *The Shepherd's Guidebook*, written by Ralph Neighbour, Jr. These are really good for groups that are just getting started.

 **uestion:** **BIBLE STUDIES IN THE CELL**

Cell groups seem to discourage doing Bible studies during the meeting. Why?

 nswer: The cell group is a time when a group of people gather to enter into God's presence, power, and purpose. While a Bible study is a wonderful thing to do, the cell meeting isn't the place to dive into God's Word and get lost in the deeper understanding of a passage for the sake of knowledge. The meeting is based on relationships, interaction, and the use of God's Word as a measuring stick and application guide for the cell members.

This doesn't mean that a grounding in God's Word is not vital to the success of your cell church! Your senior pastor is a godly person who spends hours every week preparing a message for your Sunday Celebration. He has probably been to seminary and has a firm understanding of the Old Testament and the New Testament and will interpret scripture accurately.

Your weekly cell agenda may be designed from his message text. If so, you have learned a biblical truth on Sunday and you are applying that truth to your life during your cell meeting.

In addition to your pastor's messages, *Cover The Bible* should be used to give each of your cell members a solid biblical grounding. Tapes can be recorded by your pastor to enhance the study, or you can order a set of tapes from TOUCH Outreach Ministries. Your church may also offer a deeper Bible Study class that you should attend.

Question: CELL MEMBER INVOLVEMENT

How can I involve all the members of my cell in the weekly cell meeting?

Answer: A seasoned cell leader will delegate the four W's, (Welcome, Word, Worship, and Works) to responsible members each week and break up the cell group into smaller groups during the Word and ministry portions of the meeting. This way, the preparation load is carried by many, creating ownership. A high level of communication is necessary so that the four W's fit together, but when you get accustomed to delegating and inspecting this area, it gets easier.

Breaking out into small groups gives quiet people the freedom to share. It also puts the loud or long-talking people in small groups where they can give input without dominating the whole group or meeting.

Question: **GOD'S MOVEMENT**

We don't sense God moving during our meetings. How can this be changed?

Answer: First let me note that this is not a question concerning the use of spiritual gifts in a cell meeting. Churches in every major and minor denomination sense the presence, power, and purpose of God in cell meetings. The important issue is to invite God to come and do whatever He wants. He promises His presence, yet the cell may need to wait on God with an extra song or a quiet time of meditation and prayer.

It will take patience and practice, but if you become one voice during your cell meetings and cry out for God, He will come! "Where two or more are gathered, there will I be also."

Question: **DEVIATION FROM CELL AGENDA**

Am I allowed to deviate or discard the cell agenda my leadership has provided if the Holy Spirit leads me in another direction?

Answer: You should always remain faithful to the authority God has placed above you, so discuss this question with your pastor or coach and get their answers. But it should be stated that God is in charge and His Holy Spirit may move you to change course during the meeting. With the permission of your pastor beforehand, ask the cell members present if a course correction is in order from what they sense God wants to do in your midst . . . you will receive confirmation and a blessing at the same time by involving them in the decision.

Question: HANDLING THE TALKER

We have a 70 year old cell member who tells numerous stories during cell meetings. He takes us off topic and its been difficult to really minister to each other with this situation. At meetings when he's not there, we can really sense the Holy Spirit moving deeply in our midst. We've pinpointed his storytelling as the problem. Now what do we do about it? We don't want to hurt his feelings.

Answer: There are two issues here. You have a person who talks too much in the cell and this needs to be corrected. Then there's a second issue in that he's older than you are and you don't want to hurt his feelings. Let's discuss each item separately.

Don't be too concerned with those personality types who are energetic, ever ready to visit with others, and make friends easily. They can easily be reminded to give others a chance to share and think before they speak. This type of conversation can be entered into after a cell meeting and then a reminder can be offered during the meeting if it happens again. Usually that fixes the problem. In this case, you have someone who is being temporarily insensitive and doesn't want to be that way any longer.

On the other hand, chronic talkers in a cell meeting hinder others from speaking. They either have a control issue, something to hide, or both. The best thing you can do is to confront them in love. The way to begin this process is to intercede for them when you would normally be growling internally during your cell meeting. Ask God to show you His love for these people and how to approach them.

When you do approach them, always keep their best interest at heart. If you only approach them because they are making cell meetings miserable for others, they will see no personal value in working on this problem. This is harder to do than you think, so stay "prayed up" for the task. Ask the person if you can meet with him or her to discuss an important matter (don't make light of the issue by saying it's no big deal, but you want to visit with them). Ask him if he sees anything different in his behavior during meetings compared to the rest of the group. He may say he is outspoken right away, or tell you he sees nothing different.

If he comments on how much he talks during the meeting, tell him that's exactly what you need to discuss. Ask the person if he knows why he talks so much during meetings. What you want to do is to get the person to dig down inside themselves and find the root issue. Is he hiding something? Is he afraid of "dead air" time in a group setting? Continue to ask questions until he voices the real issue. Even if you know the root issue, telling him won't solve anything. He must voice it himself in order to overcome it. When he does, pray with him and ask God to deliver him from the root issues. Then, ask him to pray and ask forgiveness as well. Finally, help him walk out new habits of listening before he speaks by having him keep an eye on you so that you can signal him when he has said enough.

If he doesn't have a clue as to what you're talking about when you ask the question "do you see anything different in your behavior in cell meetings?" you'll need to share with him that the amount of talking he does in the meeting is hurting the group's growth. Then, help him find the root issue as described above.

The second issue of not wanting to hurt someone's feelings must be examined carefully. Christians have an awful habit of avoiding one another and doing anything *except* entering into conflict. They move pews on Sunday and just avoid the other person until it dies down or they forget each other exists. This can't happen in a cell group!

If you really love someone, you'll confront him or her in love and enter into conflict. It will be painful to you for a short season, but it will help both of you grow. Don't become Satan's victim by saying "I respect Tim too much to say anything to him about his issue." The truth of the matter is that if you respect Tim, you'll go out on the emotional limb to save him from continuing a sinful lifestyle!

Question: DISRUPTIVE CELL MEMBERS

How do I handle a cell member who repeatedly continues to disrupt the cell meeting?

Answer: When a cell member continues to "throw rocks" at ideas, take us off topic repeatedly and doesn't take the normal, quiet hints, I do the following, and most of the time it works:

1. Redirect the person in the meeting where he or she made the offense. This is done gently, but very directly.

    a. I will often listen for a few minutes to make sure he or she is doing what I think they are doing.

    b. When I am sure, I quickly jab my open hand into his or her general direction with a simultaneous "Pardon the interruption, but I wanted to stop you so that we could discuss the issue at hand. Do you have anything to share from your heart on the subject? We'd love to hear that!"

(Cell leaders must view the meeting as a Sunday dinner with family. We talk over the week's events, correct the children in front of the other children, laugh, talk, pray, and minister to one another.)

2. This will probably shock or offend the person. It depends on how dense he or she is to the problem. If he looks offended or dumbfounded, I will use this as an opportunity to ask him (during the meeting) if he is open to some feedback from group members. If he agrees, turn to the cell members and ask them to give Bob some *productive* feedback (no rock throwing!). Members should be able to say things like "Bob, we really enjoy you in this cell group. But we experience you as someone who has his own agenda. We know you love us, but when you take us off topic consistently, week after week, we don't feel as if you really want to lay your life down for others."

3. After a few have shared with Bob, give him time to process and share. You may need a long, long, *long* pause of silence. This is very good! Long periods of silence allow the Holy Spirit to speak to people when they can hear and focus on Him. If Bob shares a deep need, put a chair in the middle of the room and once again, wait on God to give you and your members something to say. *Do not just pray the first thing that comes to mind.* Wait for the Spirit's guidance.

4. If Bob just starts in again with his personal agenda, stop him and ask him if he recognizes that he's doing it again. Bob has to see that his actions are habitual and have a root.

5. Bob may want ministry and may desire to find the root of his problem and work through it. If so, ask another senior member of your cell to accompany you and minister to him at his home one on one. The cell meeting will not be long enough to do this.

6. If Bob doesn't agree with anything you've said, affirm him and tell him that you love him *unconditionally*. You will need to stop him from speaking or work out an arrangement where he receives permission to speak until he is able to work through his issues *and* change the habits that he has formed to support these issues.

7. Either way, the cell must begin to fast and pray for Bob. He really needs you! God will break through in his life, and the cell will be blessed that they were a part of that. Remember, when one member hurts, the whole cell should hurt! If they don't, all they have to do is to ask God to help them understand how Bob is hurting, and God will most certainly give them a taste that will drive a concerted prayer effort.

uestion: THE DIFFICULT CELL MEMBER

Toby sits in the cell meeting and says absolutely nothing. He will answer direct questions in a few words in conversation outside of the meeting, but does not talk during meetings. Period.

Attendance? At his convenience, lateness common. On icebreakers? No news/declines to share. Sharing in the reading of a passage? He has the circle pass him over. Worship? Keeps to self, reading the lyrics. Closing prayers in a circle for the person on the right? Refuses to start. Listing of unsaved friends for intercession? Toyed with the pencil and paper that night. On scripture study? Mute.

What should I do?

Observation:

While I haven't met Toby personally, it wouldn't surprise me if he has big or numerous unresolved issues in his life. These issues have probably paved a beautiful highway for satanic strongholds, and Toby may not even know it. Or, he might know it well and as odd as it may sound, harboring these issues and supporting their ongoing validity feels better than dealing with them. Either way, Toby needs to be loved through this by you, other cell members, and maybe a Christian counselor who believes in spiritual warfare and the support of a cell group.

Answer: Assuming Toby's mom isn't dragging him to cell meetings against his will, he must feel compelled to come for some reason! It would be very good to ask him why point blank outside of a cell meeting.

What would I do with Toby if I were in your shoes?

1. Visit with him privately and ask him if he is open to personal feedback. When this meeting occurs, others in your cell should be fasting and praying for a breakthrough.

   a. If he says "No, I'm not" you must gently tell him that being a member of this cell group means being open to input and a willingness to take part in cell life. Then ask Toby if you can pray with him right now. Pray that God will reveal anything and everything that is keeping Toby from living in fellowship with other Christians. When you're finished praying, ask him to pray the same prayer. He may not do this, but you need to challenge him to do so. Praying with him this way should "turn up the heat" and cause a new work to begin in his life.

   b. If he says "Yes" you must tell him much the same as "No, I'm not." The difference is that you will know that he is verbally open to feedback. In addition to the above, you must explain to Toby about "Edification Factors."

A *Positive* Edification Factor is someone who adds to the meetings, shows up on time, opens their home for the meeting and for others to come over and be an active, ongoing part of their life, spends time with unbelievers, etc.

A *Neutral* Edification Factor is someone who attends cell frequently but adds nothing and sits there like a bump on a log. They take part in cell events, but don't work at cell life. It just happens if it happens.

A *Negative* Edification Factor is someone who shows up late, doesn't talk, or trashes the cell members and activities. This person makes others feel that they can't share openly and drags the cell down by his actions.

Ask Toby which factor fits his current actions in cell life. Wait for an answer as long as it takes. You may sit there ten minutes before he speaks! This is very important. If Toby needs to process this in his head, let him have all the time he wants.

2. This may not be the only time you meet with Toby. You may need to ask him if the cell can pray over him at the meeting next week and regularly outside of the meeting at his home.

3. You should make the supervisor or senior pastor aware of this. Always tell cell members that you cannot be bound to confidentiality, but you promise not to share deep issues with church leadership outside of their presence. This allows you to get them the help they need without them feeling that you have broken a promise or trust. Your members must also know that you may be forced to share deep issues with a church leader over you even if they did not give permission when the issue warrants it.

What Toby needs is a group of people to love him to a new place in life. I have worked with similar people that do not want help and the actions above have helped them decide to run away from those who love him or her. Other problemed people make significant changes in their life because a group of people has shown God's unconditional love to them. The key here is not to become fixated on Toby and his problems as a leader or cell. If the cell feels that their sole task is to get Toby fixed and verbal in meetings, they will tire of this quickly. There is a tender balance that must be obtained in this situation.

Developing Leaders

Developing Leaders

Q **uestion:** **SELF-STUDY EQUIPPING TRACK**

My cell members don't see a need to go through the self-study equipping track my church has designed for discipleship. How can I help them see a need for it? Our church has been transitioning for a year or so and we're doing our first groups after our prototype groups multiplied.

A **nswer:** This is one of the most difficult parts of working in a cell environment with "mature" Christians. I put the word *mature* in quotations because most believers who have been in church life for a year or more think they're mature, and they probably aren't unless they have been consistently mentored. So this may be the first problem! Your cell members may think they're mature because they've been attending church for years, and that they don't need this "elementary" equipping track.

Helping them see they aren't mature believers (see the children, young men, and fathers lessons in the *Arrival Kit* for a deeper understanding of what "mature" means) can be very offensive if you don't approach the subject right. Here's what I have learned that works if you're willing to stick with it:

1. Discuss the word "mature" one night during the Word portion of your cell meeting. Ask each member to share what they think the word mature means for believers. Let them each share their ideas, and then read the passage of scripture found in 1 John 2:12-14. Use the first few weeks of the *Arrival Kit* to prepare.

While some of your members have reached others for Jesus, they have not "overcome the evil one" as a young man or young woman (this scripture applies to both sexes!) This is much like a teenager who births or sires a baby but isn't mature enough to hold down a job and provide for the child. We wouldn't call this young person mature, just fertile!

Help each member see where they are and ask them if they are happy in that place. Most believers want to please God and grow in Him. Hopefully, none of your members will say "I know what you mean and I don't care if God wants me to mature. I'm not interested." That would be a whole different scenario.

Next, explain that your church has designed a solid way to take a spiritual "little child" and help them overcome the evil one (young man) and reproduce themselves with new Christians (father). While some have passed the "little child" into the "young man" phase, they will surely be mentoring or "sponsoring" a new Christian soon enough. The equipping track can't be offered by someone who is a stranger to it. Even the first studies, although basic, will bring newfound freedom from strongholds and a new level of maturity.

Let me also say that every time I use the TOUCH equipping track with a new Christian or cell member who I am sponsoring, God reveals Himself to me in a very special way. I learn something new about Him and deepen my walk, even doing the basics. It's not just good review for me; it helps me become consistent!

2. Go through your church's equipping track and begin today if you haven't started! Once you have finished the first book, begin to mentor your interns through it.

As your interns finish the first book, they should take at least one person under their wing and do the same. Even the unbelievers attending your cell regularly can do the equipping track. I have friends who came to Christ in the middle of using *The Arrival Kit*!

Important Note: Mentoring and equipping go together. If everyone is mentoring another in your group, the equipping will perk along if they see a need for it. Because it's difficult and there will be obstacles in completing it, you really need a close friend to lean upon. See the need for both at the same time?

Question: GROUPS OF 12

In putting together a group of twelve, should I seek twelve individuals or twelve couples? I seem to get conflicting advice on this.

Answer:

1. Don't seek a certain number of people to fill a group. Prayerfully challenge those who are most willing and able to reach the world for Jesus. As you meet on a weekly basis, help each person see their "*oikos*" and how to reach their friends, neighbors, and co-workers for Jesus. You must also spend many hours together between meetings to become "a spiritual family." This is the most powerful aspect of your ministry to your flock!

2. When a single member or a married couple have proven themselves to you repeatedly in the areas of successful evangelism, discipleship (their converts have reached unbelievers for Christ) and they have launched a group of their own that meets on a different night of the week, invite them to become a *permanent* part of your cell if you feel God's calling to do so.

3. As other group members launch new cells and reach their world for Christ, you will invite them to become part of your permanent group. Your standards must be very high for the invitation of permanent status to be extended!

4. When you have up to twelve couples (working as one) or individuals with their own groups meeting on another evening apart from your meeting with them, you will have a group of 12 and you can close it. New believers you personally reach for Christ will stay in your original group for a couple of weeks before moving into one of your member's groups.

(You may decide to close your group at 7 married couples if you feel group dynamics are suffering . . . in Bogota, some of the G12's are over 20 persons. I personally like a lower number of people because I can more effectively minister to them and keep up with their growth.)

This is the information given to us by Cesar Castillanos. Many variations on this have already been implemented by large and small churches around the world. The main thrust behind the G12 structure is that everyone is mobilized and encouraged to launch a group with new converts. This keeps the evangelism and leadership development machine running at all levels of leadership indefinitely!

uestion: AGE AND CELL LEADERSHIP

I have been praying hard about being a cell leader. I have agreed to leadership and go through my internship in my cell, but I have a concern. Everyone else in my cell is much older, wiser, and deeper in their faith than I am (they're in their 40's and 50's and I'm just 30). The leadership part doesn't scare me, but being over these seasoned veterans has made me skittish about the whole thing. Although I've been a believer since childhood, any wisdom from you for my situation would be appreciated!

Answer: I see your point! My father has told me on more than one occasion that he "has eaten more salt than I have eaten rice," which is an old Chinese saying for "respect your elders and their years of experience." Let me adjust your concept of cell leadership a bit with the following thoughts:

1. A great shepherd "leads" the sheep entrusted to him. This is earned through servanthood and prayer. When you love people by laying down your life for each of them and love them just where they are in life, they will respect you and follow you. Leadership had nothing to do with your biblical knowledge, the depth of your skills, or the rings on your trunk. It has everything to do with how often you pray for and with them, mow their lawns, baby-sit their kids or pets, make dinner for them, etc. If you can do endless favors and serve your members expecting nothing in return, they will respect you at any age and do anything you ask once you have

31

earned it. By the way, you'll have to keep up the hard work if you want to remain a "great shepherd." Stop serving and you'll lose your leadership role!

2. Never forget they are not *your* sheep! You are a faithful undershepherd for your pastor and the Lord, who have asked you to tend part of their flock in a remote pasture. This should emotionally free you if you stop and think about it! God is in charge, the buck stops with your pastor, and your main role is to lay down your life for them and make sure they get proper nourishment, protection from wolves (satan and demons), and that you keep count of the new lambs and bring them in when they are born in the fields.

Care for them as if they were your own, but never forget that someone else bought those sheep at a very high price. God wants to use ordinary people for *extraordinary* purposes with the power of the Holy Spirit. As long as you never take full ownership, you will never feel overwhelmed. Your pastor and your Lord want to make sure you succeed. You are simply protecting and loving a group of people the way Jesus would if He walked the streets of your town today.

3. Observation: If your pastor has chosen you above these mature, older Christians it may be that you are the only one among them who is faithful, able, and teachable. Cell leadership is quite challenging because the needs of others are constantly pushing you out of your comfort zone. Few Christians in America are willing to be uncomfortable for anyone, including our Lord. Look around!

Are others in your group better suited for leadership but are unwilling to make the sacrifices necessary to see it happen? Pray and fast for them. God will soften their hearts when you serve them and your lifestyle will provide contrast easily seen through actions, not words.

Question: TIME MANAGEMENT

I think I understand the responsibilities of a cell leader, but it would appear that I need 48 hours in a given day to make it all work and I'll have to quit my job or ignore my family. This can't be what you're saying, is it?

Answer: From a human perspective, it does look like a mountain of responsibility to move with a spoon, doesn't it? But that's not reality if:

1. You are called by God to be a cell leader.

2. You operate under the power of the Holy Spirit.

3. You allow your pastor to help you manage the duties of cell leadership and submit to the authority over you.

If you feel called by God to be a cell leader, you will be drawing from an energy source much greater than yourself. It is miraculous how God works through us when we are working within our calling and at the pace He desires for us. He pulls the weight of the plow, and we walk along side Him in His yoke. That's exactly how a farmer trains a new, young ox. He straps the young ox along side a seasoned older ox that knows the plow and the fields. The young ox walks the fields, in the direction and the speed of the older ox and learns how to plow . . . but not under its own power. Your calling will not always be easy, but you will succeed with a balanced lifestyle that will not wear you out if you follow God at His speed in His direction. Jesus always got everything done on His list everyday because He listened to His Master and followed His instructions! You too must spend the necessary time in prayer to receive God's instructions on the use of your time and abilities.

Your role as a cell leader is to pastor a small part of the flock for God and for your pastoral leadership. You should adopt the members of your cell as your own sheep, but never forget that you are a faithful undershepherd for your pastor and the Lord. If you feel stressed and overwhelmed with your role and duties as a cell leader, take time out to pray and ask God what to do — you will receive revised marching orders! The Lord may give you insight concerning your attitudes about family, your job, and the use of your time.

Here's an idea to help you sort out your multi-faceted life. List all the tasks you do on a weekly basis and how much time you must invest in each of them to do them well. Then, pray and ask the Lord to give you an understanding of the tasks you should delegate to others in your cell and the tasks that you could overlap (ie. exercise and spend time with your kids; go to the warehouse grocery with unsaved friends on Saturday morning, etc.)

If this doesn't relieve the stress of leadership, make an appointment with your zone supervisor or pastor. He or she is more than willing to help you make tough decisions and see where you might have misunderstood your role as a cell leader. While you may not like everything you hear, God pours blessings upon His people when they are submissive and willing to make changes in their personal lives and habits to reach the world for Jesus.

Question: LACK OF COMMITMENT

Why doesn't anyone want to be an cell leader intern in my group?

Answer: There are many answers to this question. It might be that no one feels they are ready for the role. Or it may be that they have been watching you and don't want all the headaches you have!

You may wince at this statement, but it's often the case. If your members hear your gripes about the responsibility and see the bags under your eyes from all the work you do with no apparent reward, it's no wonder they don't want the role. Share the joys of cell leadership with them as often as possible. Gripe about issues and problems with your zone supervisor or pastor. This doesn't mean you should shield them from the difficult areas of leadership, but make sure to show the good before the bad!

The other reason most cell members don't want to become cell leaders is that they don't have a vision for the task at hand. If you cast this vision for them by giving them responsibilities occasionally and involving them in the decision making process of cell life and growth, they will be better prepared when your church has a retreat for prospective cell leaders.

Question: **LEADERSHIP QUALITIES**

I see wonderful leadership qualities in one of my cell members, but he lives well beyond his means and he is in debt over his head. Should this person be considered for cell leadership anyway?

Answer: If your cell member wants to rectify the problem by changing his spending habits and paying off the bills with a second job, he won't have time to be a good cell leader for the duration. If he doesn't see a problem with living the high life on a low income, he really isn't mature enough to be a good leader for existing cell members and new Christians who will look to him as an example.

Question: LEADING THE OPPOSITE SEX

I'm a married man with a woman as a cell leader intern. How can I make this work?

Answer: This scenario requires your wife to co-lead the cell with you and train the female intern. You should never meet with the female intern alone or speak to her on the phone at length without your wife involved in the conversation on an extension phone. Satan will use this opportunity to destroy your ministry if he is given one open door. Guard your hearts and your minds against schemes of the Devil!

This should not prevent you from moving forward. Make it very plain to the female intern that your wife will be spending a vast majority of the time with her for training. You may join them anytime, but you will never meet with the intern alone. If you, your spouse, the female intern or her husband (if she is married) are uncomfortable in the least way with this arrangement, visit with your zone supervisor or pastor and allow the female intern to complete her training in another cell or wait until your cell multiplies.

By the way, this is a great place to mention that when a cell member agrees to become a cell leader, his or her spouse must be enthusiastic, supportive, and willing to co-lead. Anything less is a recipe for failure, unless you are grooming them for a men or women only group.

Question: MINISTRY TO PEOPLE OF THE OPPOSITE SEX

Should I do a Journey Guide Interview alone with a person of the opposite sex?

Answer: No.

Always bring a second person along with you, preferably someone who is the same sex as the cell member. Your husband or wife would work well if you are married. And, you should bring this person's new sponsor or mentor along with you.

Ask the cell member being interviewed if he or she is comfortable sharing the contents of the *Journey Guide*. If he or she is not willing, send his or her new sponsor with a mature believer in your cell that is the same sex and has completed *The Arrival Kit*.

Question: ACCOUNTABILITY IN THE CELL

How can I get my members to see the importance of accountability partnerships and the equipping track my church has designed for discipleship?

Answer: If someone has ever been in a productive accountability relationship with a close friend or mentor, he will tell you it was the most powerful time in his life. God's Word states that "iron sharpens iron" and we must hold each other accountable if we want to see spiritual growth and maturity.

It all begins with you. If you meet weekly with your cell leader intern, you can help him or her move from cell member to cell leader. He or she too should be helping a cell member move from immaturity to maturity in all aspects of the Christian walk. Your testimony about this time together during your meetings will plant seeds of encouragement.

Next, meet with your supervisor and ask him or her to help you make a strategy as to what partnerships would be the most productive. (Many of the best accountability partnerships are between two or three people of the same sex that aren't life-long friends.)

Then, ask each member of each partnership if they would be willing to meet with you and their partner(s) for a meeting. In this meeting, explain that your cell is committed to reaching the lost and bringing maturity to the cell members. Your church has a solid strategy for doing this successfully, but it will require that the partnerships meet weekly and cover basic questions surrounding the Christian walk. Your questions may be different, but here are a few that are heavily used and insightful:

1. Have you spent the necessary time God needs to have with you in your quiet time and in His Word?

2. What has He been saying to you this week about your walk with Him, your earthly and spiritual family, your job, and the unbelievers in your life?

3. This week have you surrendered to a sinful habit that you cannot control?

4. What insights have you found as you have walked through the material in the equipping track?

5. Have you lied or shaded the truth about anything we've discussed?

Explain to the partnerships that they must step out on faith and make this weekly time a priority. Then, help them determine a time and place where they will meet regularly. It can be at someone's home, a coffee shop or restaurant, or in the parking lot of an office building before work.

The last piece of advice is the best way to solve this problem. Accountability partnerships are truly a stop-gap measure for cell members who do not have new Christians to disciple. When your cell is successful in reaching the lost for Jesus, everyone will have the privilege of sponsoring a new convert and will be thrilled with the opportunity!

Entering into Community

Entering into Community

Question: SMALL GROUP VS CELL GROUP

How can I help all my church members who are now in cells in an understanding that a "cell group" is different from our previous small groups?

Answer: I received the following "crowd breaker" from a fellow in a transitioning cell church. Use this in your cell group to help your whole cell understand the difference between a "inward" looking fellowship group or Bible study and an evangelistic "outward" looking cell group:

1. At the beginning of your meeting, ask everyone to stand in a circle. (Make sure you don't have a coffee table in the middle of the circle or it will mess up this exercise.)

2. Ask one person in your cell to stand a few feet outside the circle alone.

3. Ask everyone in the circle to join hands or link arms. Everyone should take one step toward the middle of the circle "after" you say the following:

    a. "A Home Group (or whatever you used to call your old

groups) loves to meet together for Bible reading and prayer."

b. "Home Group members appreciate the support they give other members when they meet together."

c. "Home Groups are very familiar with other members because they've been together for years."

4. While everyone is packed tightly in a small circle, ask the "outsider" how he or she feels right now and if one could join the group as they physically see it.

5. Ask the group to look at the outsider without breaking the tightly knit circle. (Many will strain as they try to turn their neck around to view the person.) Ask the members if it was hard to see the outsider in this all-too-comfortable situation.

6. Now reform the group (with the outsider intact) as a cell group by asking all the members to put their left hand in the middle of the circle (like a baseball team would do for a team cheer).

7. Tell the group that each *cell* member gathers together each week to link up as the body of Christ in the *welcome* part of the meeting.

8. Then ask everyone to raise their right hand above their head, which symbolizes *worship*.

9. Now, ask everyone to turn their left hand over to expose their palms (with everyone still touching hands), representing the *word* portion of the meeting where we apply God's Word to our lives.

10. Last, explain that the meeting never ends because of the outstretched right hand in the *works* portion (ask everyone to do this) which symbolically allows us to draw in visitors while remaining in community.

11. Finally, ask the "outsider" how he or she feels about this new grouping, whether one could easily join in, and what's attractive about it. Ask the group members how it feels to relate together and outsiders this way and if they see a new contrast.

Thanks to Mike Shorah, a pastor at Holy Trinity in Hazlemere, United Kingdom for this.

Question: BECOMING FAMILY

I call every member of my cell once a week and touch base with them. I pray for them daily too. It just seems like they don't care enough about cell life to actually become family like you teach. What should I do?

Answer:

Typically, this scenario happens in churches where traditional Christians have been in church life for years and have deeply rooted friendships. These people don't need community with their cell members because they already have it with a couple of other Christians and they're content. But they don't realize that they must form a family-type relationship with other members or they will never see the cell grow and multiply or experience personal growth.

Read Acts 2:42-47 in the Word portion of your next cell meeting. Go around the room and ask every person to answer a couple of important questions:

1. What kind of lifestyle did the people in Acts maintain?

2. Is there a difference in your current lifestyle and what you see in this passage?

Now it's time for ministry! Break up into small groups of four or into accountability/sponsor-sponsee partnerships and allow your members to discuss their feelings and current lifestyle. Then ask every person to pray for total abandonment of any lifestyle that hinders reaching the lost through community within your cell.

You must also model community for them. Ask them to come over to your house to eat a meal or watch a ball game or movie together. Ask them to do favors for you that are somewhat inconvenient for them. Now you "owe them one" and they will feel free to ask a returned favor. This is one good way to get the community ball rolling.

While calling your cell members weekly is a great thing to do, get into every member's home as often as you can to make an impact on them.

- Find out who their friends are and ask if you can meet them.
- Make a date to take care of your member's kids and give them a free night away from the house.
- Use "active" listening skills when you visit with them and find out what their interests are and what their friendships are based upon.

Finally, praying and fasting for "purpose-driven community" is the most powerful thing and the first thing you should do. God will reveal His unique ways and methods to you and nothing is better than that!

Question: THE ROLE OF PROPHECY

I have a new Christian in my cell group who is scripturally untaught, but claims to be a prophet. He claims that he cannot control his sudden "prophetic" outbursts and he feels like he is speaking the words of God. This disturbs the other cell members. What role does the gift of prophecy play in the cell? Should I allow this to continue? And how should I handle it?

Answer: In some churches, prophecy is very much a part of cell group life. In other churches, the manifestation gifts are not as obvious (it all depends on the doctrinal stance you, your church, and/or denomination holds). Prophetic words are always judged by the group and leadership when they are shared. Prophesy must also align with God's Word.

Prophecies like "Quit your job and move to Montana where you will find a man named Ben. You will marry him and have three children, one boy and two girls" are best shared in private and reviewed by a pastoral staff member.

This should be stopped if it is disruptive and you feel it is unhealthy for your group. Ask him to share these prophetic words with a pastor on staff *before* he shares them in your cell group. If he's truly sharing prophetic things, your pastor needs to hear it too! Remember that the spirit of the prophet is subject to the prophet. Therefore, he should practice self-control.

If I were you I'd get my pastor or coach involved immediately. Call a meeting with this man and your pastor. In the meeting, briefly share your concern and then sit back and watch what happens next. Your pastor will help you handle it. There are two issues here. The first is the content of this man's words and the second is his disruptive delivery of that content. Both must be addressed, but the man may not see the difference between the two and this will take some processing. Watch and learn!

Question: MARKETING SCHEMES

> After a recent cell meeting, one of my interns (who sells dietary supplements through a multi-level marketing company) was speaking with members in the group about the products he sells and the advantages, etc. I feel uneasy about this. I don't want to give my intern the impression that I want to keep him from making extra money and helping folks with a healthy product. But, I don't want things to get out of control either. What guidelines should I follow in this situation?

Answer: I've lost a few cell members and budding leaders to multi-level marketing (MLM) schemes. Some of these organizations are Christian-based, and folks come to Christ at their regional rallies. This makes it even harder to rationally discuss the drawbacks of the time involvement that would have been invested in cell life when discussing the pitfalls and true time requirements for this kind of 'part time' work.

I have been approached many times to take on a second, part time job selling something through an MLM. I could probably make an extra five or ten thousand a year doing this, but it would completely take me away from my primary task in life, which is reaching people for Jesus and showing them how to do the same! I would rather do without the extra money and see my friends come to Jesus.

It's important to always remember to "keep the main thing the main thing." Successful cell groups (those people that band together, reach lost friends and family for Jesus, and raise up leaders from within) don't invest all their free time in making extra money. They get out of debt and stay debt free. They live within their means. They change jobs if the work is too demanding on their time and keeps them from cell life. They understand that "quality family time" means sharing lots of evenings with other families because it builds the Kingdom.

Let me temper these comments with this. I understand that many Christians have basic financial needs and must provide for their families. But I personally feel that cell groups should have one focus and one focus only . . . making disciples!

What did I do when my own intern started networking with my members for his MLM two years ago? I quickly approached him in love and told him that I understood he needed to make a living for his family. I clearly stated that interaction with our group should be to edify, encourage, and help them win people for Jesus, not draw them into a second job that would destroy the cell life we had worked so hard to cultivate. He retorted numerous times that his 'program' was Christian-based and that many people came to Christ when they discovered the MLM's brand of 'financial freedom.' But I was firm and told him to find his new business partners outside of the cell structure of our church (my senior pastor and I met with him to tell him this.)

He and his wife left our cell to do their MLM on evenings and weekends. They struggled with us for a while, but the time slots needed for their side job crowded out cell life and our weekly meetings. Where are they today? They have abandoned the MLM and are back in a cell church as cell leaders. They, like millions of other people who have tried an MLM, found that nothing comes easily. Few stay in them because the income only grows when friends and family distribute and personally use the products and enroll others.

Bottom line: Help your entrepreneurial cell member understand that God designed him for a special purpose. There is room for earning a living, but not at the expense of using the gifts and talents God gave him to reach the lost for Jesus and disciple them to do the same thing!

**uestion:** **BUILDING NEW RELATIONSHIPS IN THE GROUP**

I am presently sponsoring (mentoring) a friend and we have begun our church's equipping track for members. My husband is sponsoring my friend's husband. They have been coming to our cell for a few weeks now. We want to see them establish other relationships to help them become rooted in our cell church. I wouldn't want them to feel like they can only come to us when they have needs. Is their any way to help encourage them to be building new relationships within the group?

nswer: There are numerous ways to help your new cell members/close friends build relationships with other cell members and even your cell church at large:

1. Hold regular game nights (a party mixer to get folks talking and laughing together over card or board games in a home environment). These should be focused as non-threatening events to connect to the lost, but the planning and strategy of a game night involves numerous people in the group. Ask your new members to help a seasoned cell member plan the evening. This way, they will become team members and learn to serve along with others.

2. Make sure they are repeatedly invited to the Sunday services of your church by every member of the cell. If you can sit together as a cell group at the Celebration each week, they will come back because they have a strong comfort zone around them with people

they know well. From the first minute they walk in the door of the church building on Sunday introduce them to people, especially the senior pastor and staff of your church. This makes them feel welcome and a part of something much bigger.

3. Ask a mature member of your cell to join you for your weekly accountability time with this new member. As a trio, you can help her see that discipleship isn't so much one-on-one as it is learning from many and being a part of a family . . . a spiritual family!

4. The *Journey Guide* interview reveals many things about a person, but it also clues you into his or her hobbies. Make a careful note about this and see if any other cell members have the same or a similar hobby. There's a friendship in the making if you can find common ground. I do this with my own hobby of marine aquariums, and I've deepened relationships with cell members and unbelievers alike.

uestion: HEALTHY CELLS

How can I tell if I have a healthy cell?

nswer: There are six kinds of people in a healthy cell group. I've listed each with a brief description:

1. A strong cell leader (and his or her spouse, if it's a family group, where the spouse is participative, not just supportive) that cares to the point of personal sacrifice, and who has made the members of his or her group *real* friends or adopted family. This cell leader (and spouse) is faithful to the vision of his local church and senior pastor and attends all the training events and monthly meetings where he can be continually challenged to succeed in cell leadership. He has a strong desire to see the lost won to Christ and to raise up new leaders from within his or her group.

2. At least one new cell leader undergoing the internship process (and his or her participative spouse, if it's a family group) who helps facilitate meetings, calls on and prays with members during the week, and works hard to take ownership of the group from the leader over the course of the cell cycle. This budding leader also has a strong desire to see the lost won for Christ, and is actively looking for or developing an "intern" of his or her own when the existing group multiplies.

3. Spiritual "fathers and mothers" who are firm in their faith and who are mentoring or sponsoring other cell members. They aren't bound by satanic strongholds and they can be called a father or mother because they have brought and will continue to bring others to Christ. While the cell leader and interns would also be in this category, this group is where a cell finds new leaders. They're ready for the challenge.

4. Spiritual "young men and women" who have overcome the evil one (who have sought and found freedom from satanic strongholds) and are developing their *oikos* of unbelievers to win them to Christ, with the other members of the cell group. These people are probably mentoring or sponsoring "little children" and will disciple those whom they reach for Christ.

5. Spiritual "little children" who have never been discipled to the point where they can overcome obstacles in God's vision for their lives. This term also covers Christians who join a cell group and have crippling problems (emotional, spiritual, financial). These issues are usually the sole focus of the immature believer, and he or she cannot see beyond individual hurts or issues to minister to others or reach the lost for Christ.

6. The unsaved visitor is also a vital part of a healthy cell group. These folks are there because a group member has invited them. They may have some religious background, or it may all be brand new to them. These people provide both sparks of life and opportunities for unconditional love and acceptance by other group members. They are learning much about God, but drag the world's opinions, practices, attitudes, and values into your group.

Your cell is a healthy group if you and your spouse are in the lives of your members and visitors, you have new leaders coming up and serving the group regularly, and your group is inviting the lost into your lives and weekly meetings. If you're praying for the lost and they're showing up, you'll have new Christians soon enough and they'll require discipleship and mentoring.

Hurting cell members (#5) are a sign of health, even if you wish you didn't have any! They give you ample reason to cry out to God in prayer for miracles and solutions to their deep problems and issues. Prayer must be a foundation of your group for success, and sometimes God allows you to have hurting people in your group to force you to pray more and rely on Him, not your own wisdom.

I believe a "balanced" group would have all of the six categories of people in it, but that rarely happens! Most cell groups in the United States have interns and lots of "little children" because we've been raised in a church culture void of basic Christian community. What you must do is to pray hard, challenge your cell members to accept their call in life as a believer to build the kingdom, and share the love of Jesus as often as you can.

Your cell should be balanced as well. If you have too many "spiritual children" that are not maturing and moving forward, you'll flounder. I've also seen unbalanced groups of spiritual fathers and mothers who have a zillion toddlers (physical children, not spiritual) in their group and they can't manage all the needs of these kids. Imbalance can take many forms.

Cell design is really important, and as a cell leader, you should take a very active roll in the makeup of your cell group when it is formed each cell cycle. If your group has too many of any one of the categories above, it will suffer. Even if you have a group of solid leaders, you'll have an unhealthy situation if you think about it. The way people grow is to give away what they know. Each cell cycle, the multiplying groups should be looked at critically to insure they are formed with the right people makeup and chemistry.

Reaching Out

Reaching Out

Question: **MY CELL IS NOT GROWING**

My cell has terrific community. We make lots of phone calls and hang out with each other on weekends. Our cell meetings are great too . . . no one wants to leave when we're done. Our problem is that our cell is not growing with new converts and some of my members are balking about being equipped with daily studies and retreats. What should I do?

Answer: This is a very common problem in transitioning cell churches. The cell members understand fellowship and "one another" ministry in a small group format, but they aren't unified in a passion to see their friends, relatives, neighbors, and co-workers come to know Jesus as Savior.

This is a multi-faceted problem that will require a multi-faceted solution. Here are the steps to making your cell a healthy, disciple-making group:

1. Pray! Drop down to your knees and ask God to reveal His heart and yours as a cell leader. Current research has shown that

cell leaders who pray at least 30 minutes a day multiply groups. Those who don't pray fervently on a daily basis rarely see their group grow.

This will accomplish many things. You will see God's heart, and you will see how you must model the life of a disciple to see others in your group do the same. The more you pray, the more deeply you will understand what God wants and how He will orchestrate your life by showing you what you need to do with your time.

2. Visit each cell family individually. As a cell leader, you should schedule a time when you can go to the home of each of your members and discuss the vision of the cell. Here is where you will hear the concerns and complaints about being a "purpose-driven community of believers." Work through these issues with them and help them see how God wants to use them. You will be doing lots of listening during this time, so fight the desire to do all the talking.

You may also hear that they are very excited about evangelism efforts and just don't know how to go about it or make friends with lost people. This refreshing time for you should be an indication that you just need to mentor them and show them how it's done! Invite them to a gathering of your unbelievers, and ask them to reciprocate.

3. Pray some more! Refocus your cell by taking a half an hour to pray for a heart for the lost and then lost people in your "*oikos*". Pray this way for every week for a month or more until you see a breakthrough. Do this just after worship time, so your cell members will know that the main purpose of your cell is not to have deep relationships, but to form deep relationships to impact the world. There's a big difference.

4. Make a "Blessing List." Get a large poster board and take the names of two unbelievers from each person's "*oikos*" and write their names on this board. Use large letters at the top that state it's a "blessing list." This is important because you will bring it to every

cell meeting and give it prominent placement. Should one of the people show up on that blessing list, they will be completely taken back that a group of strangers prayed for God's blessing upon them.

5. Invite, Invite, Invite! The best way to make your cell meetings evangelistic is to invite those on your blessing list to come to parties, church events, cell meetings, etc. The more people you invite, the faster your cell will grow.

When unbelievers show up, introduce them as "friend." This will let the members know they must shift into evangelistic mode. Your icebreaker will be a history question (where did you grow up, how many brothers and sisters do you have, etc.) and a name introduction. Your worship must be very simple (have song sheets handy at all times) and someone should give a brief testimony of what God has done in their life because of a willingness to follow Him during worship.

There's a significant debate between various cell churches as to whether a cell should totally shift the meeting from an edification time to a simple "get to know you" time when unbelievers are present. Some say it's better to gear the whole meeting to the unbeliever and others say that when an unbeliever sees the power of God and the fervency of the members in prayer and ministry, they see how much they need God. I think you will have to try both and see what works best for you, the unbeliever in your midst, and the leading of the Holy Spirit.

As the cell leader you should ask everyone to bow their heads for a closing prayer at the end of the meeting. After everyone is ready, tell the group that you are going to pray a simple prayer inviting God to come into your life (as if you were praying the sinner's prayer). Then, before you dismiss the group, ask anyone who prayed that prayer for the first time to visit with you after the meeting.

Follow up with any new converts and assign them a sponsor from the natural relationships made in your cell.

The process of shifting an inward group of believers outward can take many months if you are not praying fervently for this to happen. Satan has created strongholds in their lives to keep them quiet, and you can expect spiritual warfare, prayer walking, and fasting to be a part of your breakthrough. No one said that storming the gates of hell to set captives free was going to be easy!

Question: **IDEAS FOR OUTREACH EVENTS**

I'm a cell leader and I have run out of ideas for outreach events. Any ideas?

Answer: The best way to get ideas is to involve your whole cell in the brainstorming. Each member will come up with a good idea if you pray together and ask God to reveal His plans to you. You can't do it alone and succeed! Also, when you involve the whole group in brainstorming and planning, the desire to bring unbelievers to these cell outreach events is much higher. Here's some starter ideas . . . I'm sure you'll use them to springboard even better outreach events!

- Always have something fun for the kids to do and an adult to help them do it. When parents have a good time and their kids have a better time, everyone wants to come back or visit a cell group!
- *Never* just tell the unbelievers where the party or event will be held. It's too scary to show up at a stranger's house! Arrange to

pick them up or meet them at their house and caravan together. If you caravan, make sure people from each party ride in different vehicles. The party can start as soon as you get under way!

- You will have to invite some people six times before they show up to a non-threatening event like a barbecue, game night, etc. Tell your cell members this and don't get discouraged. Also, try to invite six times as many people as you want to be there . . . the worst thing that can happen is that they all show and you have to make a run to the store for more chips and soda!

- A half night of prayer is usually necessary before events to focus the group and to do some spiritual warfare. If you've ever been to a "outreach" where no unbelievers showed up, you know what I mean.

- Some of your unbelievers may show up at your house with a bottle of alcohol. Usually when only one person drinks alcohol or sees that they'll be flying solo, they won't open it up. I have attended events where unbelievers showed up with a bottle of wine and they had a glass, but no one got drunk. I don't know what your convictions are about alcohol, so let your conscience be your guide. Just don't ruin a perfect opportunity to offer unconditional love to an unbeliever who does not live by your adopted biblical standards. Remember, they're not Christians yet, so don't expect them to live like one right away.

- Evangelism in cell groups is all about relationships, not preaching at people. If you have a meal and want to say a blessing over the people, the home, and the food, 95% of your unbelievers will enjoy it and respect it. But I wouldn't suggest a Bible Study or open sharing time when the unbelievers present expected to have a "normal" evening with new friends. If you've ever been invited to someone's home for a meal and they hammered you for an hour about their new side business with a multi-level marketing company you know exactly how unbelievers feel when you do the "bait and switch" routine on them. Apply the Golden Rule and you'll do just fine!

GAME NIGHT

Sounds hokey to some, but board and card games have become very popular again and adults love the opportunity to get to know neighbors and friends this way. If you choose to do this, make it strategic by prayerfully finding the right home, choosing the right games and the amount of time each group will play a game (I like 30 minute sessions and then rotation to other people and games). Also, make a list of who will be invited at least four weeks prior to the event. Doing this regularly every month or so on a night other than cell night will make regulars out of some of your friends.

PICNIC IN THE PARK

Each cell member should chip in five dollars for the meat. One person should be in charge of cooking. Every family will also bring a side dish and make enough food for one other family. Invite another family and plan the event when the weather is nice in your area. You should also have secondary plans if it rains or gets nasty outside . . . don't let foul weather ruin your party!

SUPERBOWL PARTY

Actually, any televised event will work, so if hockey, soccer, rugby, or baseball fits better in your cell and more importantly in the lives of your unbelieving friends, so be it. The key here is to get the biggest TV or video projector in the best host home for the event. A dinky TV will be a real letdown. And don't forget to have really good food.

ZOO PARTY

Take the whole cell and their friends to the local zoo. You may also want to have a picnic. This is especially good for cells with children.

PIZZA AND MOVIES

This is a more intimate event involving one family from your cell and an unchurched family. Rent a decent movie and order pizza when everyone gets there. Relax and spend the evening together.

LAUNDRY PARTY

This is an odd but good idea for Saturday morning. Ask another family to come over and bring their laundry and soap. Do your laundry together and watch a movie or just talk.

"GO TO MARKET" GET TOGETHER

Hey, if you have to go to the store to buy food for the week, do it with an unbeliever! Find out when they do their weekly shopping and go with them. Go to their store at their time. If it costs a little more or is out of the way, you have made a supreme sacrifice for kingdom building! This works great because someone can watch the kids or they can play together at one home. You never know . . . you might just find a tag/garage sale on the way and have to stop and take a look!

HOME FIX-UP HELPERS

If you can't get unbelievers to let you serve them, then ask them to help you do something that really makes them feel like a brother. Ask them for a *big* favor. Tell them you need them to help you and a couple of buddies (cell members) dig up flower beds at your house, build a deck, install a water heater, paint a room, move furniture, etc. Basically, anything that makes you really sweat is a big favor. Believe it or not, unbelievers think this is cool . . . you only ask "good" friends to help you do this, and then you'll owe them a *big* favor. Just remember to follow through on the favor and bring some extra muscle from your cell to help them when they have a project or need. I have added five helpers to move an unbelieving friend's stuff from apartment to apartment before, and the person was very impressed. Needless to say, they visited a cell a couple of weeks later.

What's The Bottom Line Here?

If you want to be evangelistic, involve people in your life and get into their lives. Force yourself to do it and schedule time with them and soon enough it will be a normal part of your value system. When it's appropriate, tell them what God is teaching you and that you actually hear God and know He hears you when you pray or talk to him because you have established "a connection." Use these ideas to forge relationships where this kind of conversation can happen in the future. Most people come to Christ because they know the messenger very well and have heard the message numerous times.

Question: **"OIKOS" EVANGELISM**

Our cell hasn't seen anyone saved from our "oikos" in a long, long time. We all talk about our commitment to evangelism, but we aren't successful. What should I do?

Answer: It may seem obvious, but the number one problem concerning cell-based evangelism is a simple one. Invite your unbelieving friends to cell every week until they show up!

Unbelievers visit cells because they know they are lost and are searching, or because they respect the Christian who invited them. Many cell members are afraid to invite their unbelieving friends to cell because they are sure they will be turned down or they will destroy a relationship by badgering a friend who isn't ready. While this may be true in some cases, God has placed unbelievers in the lives of Christians to make His love known! Rely on God to sustain the relationships, and expect unbelievers to turn you down and make excuses.

Most new Christians in cell groups will tell you that they were invited consistently for weeks or months before they agreed to visit a cell. So you must maintain a friendship that shows God's unconditional love for them and pray for a willing heart on a daily basis.

When you invite a lost person to your cell and they finally agree to come with you, do the following to make the evening special for them:

1. Call the host home and tell them you are bringing a guest.

2. Make sure the facilitator of the meeting knows an unbeliever will be present and that extra ice breakers will be used to make the stranger in your midst feel comfortable.

3. Sing simple songs with a single printed sheet so the unbeliever can follow along and not feel left out.

4. A cell member should share his or her one minute testimony during the worship time to give the unbeliever an understanding of what "being lost" is. Remember: You can't get find God until you know you're lost without Him!

5. The "Works" portion of the meeting should be devoted to another cell member sharing the John 3:16 diagram found in the *Touching Hearts Guidebook*. The person sharing the diagram should ask everyone to bow their head and pray. The person should pray the sinner's prayer ("God, I know my sin has set me apart from a relationship with you, and that you sent your Son Jesus to die for me and take my sin. Thank you for entering my life and becoming my best friend and Master.") Then the person should ask that anyone praying that prayer for the first time tonight should simply raise their hand. The person facilitating this part of the meeting

should visit with the new Christian and the person who brought them after the meeting.

6. Give the new Christian a copy of *Welcome To Your Changed Life* and schedule a time in the next few days when you as the cell leader and their friend can get together and talk.

Question: NEIGHBORHOOD COMMUNITY

We're in a bedroom community in a suburban area of a large city. At night, people come home from work, press the button on the garage door opener, pull in their car and go inside. They don't come out to meet their neighbors, and these are some of the most anti-social people I've encountered! How can I get to know the people who live around me to build relationships and see them come to Christ?

Answer: This is a common problem in our society. The combination of cable TV and attached garages in suburbia have made the "friendly neighbor" a thing of the past. Making the assumption that your neighbors will rarely ask to borrow a tool or cup of sugar, here are a few ideas to get into their lives:

1. Prayerwalk the streets in your neighborhood on a daily basis. Since we all need exercise, walking around the block a few times is

good for you. While you're walking, ask God to open doors in each of the homes you pass. Ask Him for an opportunity to serve or be served by the families inside. Prayerwalking is also spiritual warfare, so do not neglect to ask God to do battle in the heavenlies for freedom in your area. Boldly proclaim to the satanic forces at work in your neighborhood that you have reclaimed the area for God through the shed blood of Jesus.

[I have seen *unbelievable* results by just doing this every day for a week or two. Try it!]

2. As I stated in #1, if your neighbors don't ask you for favors, then ask them to serve you in some way! The idea is just to get the ball rolling by doing favors and helping one another to create a friendship. While your first request should not be a 5 a.m. ride to the local airport, a request to help you move a couch, get advice on a garden project, or borrow a tool (returned promptly and clean) will give them the feeling that they have done you a favor and you "owe them one." Now you can invite them over for a barbecue or pizza to thank them. The bigger the request you make, the more likely it is that they will allow you to repay them in some way.

[Note: This works best after you have prayed for them daily for at least two weeks. Some folks warm up to neighbors fast, others will take some time because they have lots of hurts, secrets to hide, or they've had lousy neighbors before you came along].

3. Get up very early Saturday morning and mow your next doors neighbor's lawn if they aren't a garden nut. You'll know they will appreciate it because they don't get around to it as often as they'd like. My next door neighbor told me this meant a lot to him. Remember to mow, edge, sweep and really do it well if you're going to do it. THEN, do your own lawn. Mowing their lawn first will help them see that you care about them more than yourself, and that this act of kindness was not an afterthought.

4. Hold an old-fashioned "ice cream social" at your home. A staff member distributed a flyer to every home on his block in person

and invited every family to bring their favorite flavor of ice cream over with the whole family from 7:00-8:30 on a Sunday night. Believe it or not, over half the block showed up! Some said this was a great excuse to meet the neighbors, others said they had the same floor plan and wanted to know how he and his wife decorated to get ideas. This ice cream social "broke the ice" and gave way to the next idea for my staff member.

5. Touch a felt need of the people on your street. During the ice cream social, my staff member looked at all the small children and realized that parenting classes would be greatly appreciated. He then asked each neighbor if this interested them and took a number of parents through a parenting class that covered a number of weeks. What needs are there on *your* block?

Question: **NO DESIRE FOR EVANGELISM**

I have cell members that have no unbelievers in their "oikos" and no real desire to share the Gospel. How do I help them?

Answer: Start by loving them enough to challenge them. Make a visit to their homes and ask them about their commitment to evangelism and discipleship. Many carnal Christians will tell you they don't feel God's call to do this and it's someone else's responsibility, but this is simply fear or an unwillingness to let go of strongholds that keep them from being soul winners. Even the most timid and shy person can be a soul winner if he or she is excited about Jesus and the freeing power of the cross!

Prior to this meeting, you should pray and fast for the cell member. Ask God to give him a willing heart and to open the floodgate of joy for his own salvation. People always share things that are exciting to them!

uestion: MOTIVATION FOR EVANGELISM

How can I help motivate my group to do evangelism (i.e. bring their friends to the group and reach out)? We have the time where we encourage them to do evangelism during our cell but some seem to be more concerned about their own needs. I know I have to be an example here but are there any other ways you have encouraged cells to evangelize?

nswer: There are lots of ways to help your cell members become soul-winners, and all begin with prayer and a heightened sense of the needs of your members.

Begin to fast and pray for your members today. Begin with one day a week as I have done. Recently I decided to fast every Monday at 9 PM to Tuesday at 9 PM. My cell gathers in a home on Tuesdays at 7 PM. I fast and then eat with them in fellowship after the meetings.

71

Why is this powerful?

Fasting generates a gnawing in your gut that reminds you to pray. You have denied yourself a basic need of human existence to see spiritual results. God honors this big time. He will send His Holy Spirit to your members as you pray for them, burdening them for the lost and diminishing their desire to focus solely on themselves.

After you have done this a for a few weeks, share it during your cell group meeting. Ask them to join you. Call them on the phone before they fast and begin to pray with them. Ask God to penetrate their hearts and minds for His purposes.

Then, get to know their unbelieving friends through social events. This way, *you* can invite them to the next cell meeting. Remember your goal in life as a cell leader: help every person in your group get a friend, family member or co-worker, saved in the next six months. By making this your goal, you will see lots of ministry needs and ways to serve them.

Also, remember that there is balance between evangelism efforts and internal ministry to your group. If a member is really hurting over something, he or she will probably be too focused to reach out. When they experience a little relief, freedom, or victory over the issue (or a sense that they're not alone in the process) they can and should get involved in evangelism. I've found that a hurt or wound heals faster when we get on with our purpose in life, which is to reconcile man to God.

PS — Many times, believers don't care about reaching the lost because they have spiritual strongholds and they need deliverance. If your church doesn't offer a deliverance weekend for cell members, ask your pastor to create this kind of environment. Christians don't have to walk this earth all bound up!

Question: INWARD-FOCUSED WARNING SIGNS

What are some of the main warning signs to watch for that would indicate a cell is becoming too inward focused?

Answer: I've listed the main warning signs, each with a short description and "way out":

Warning Sign #1 — The Cell Leader isn't living the vision. I've always found that when a cell is looking inward, the cell leader should also look in the mirror and see what has not been done that created or continued this situation. If you do not take generous portions of your weekly meetings to share the vision (see x number of new believers and three interns added by September of 2001, for example) and pray for the lost, it probably won't happen. If a cell leader doesn't report his or her struggles and breakthroughs with unbelieving friends, the group members won't see any modeling by their leader. The best thing to do is begin living it yourself, involve others, and pray for the lost every meeting. Also, change your focus on your members. Tell them you want to help them get their friends and family who live in town saved. Be their partner and challenge them to work with you this way. If they're long term "sit and soak" traditional church people who are now in a cell group, they will probably marvel at your love for them to do this.

Warning Sign #2 — The members have lost their passion for the lost. This is easy to see because they don't care about praying for the lost, and they don't talk to you about their lost friends. This is usually caused by a lack of prayer for the lost . . . God always creates a hunger. Pray individually with members in their homes about evangelism and ask them what's keeping them from seeing results.

In a variety of ways, they will tell you they have no passion, are too busy, or have one stronghold or another that is blinding them. Expect conflict when you challenge your members to reach the lost. Satan really hates it when you do this and he'll pull out all the stops to run you off.

Warning Sign #3 — You've been in the community stage of cell life for more than three months. Your cell is stuck. This rut is a hard one to get out of because Christians have been attempting to create and stay in community for the sake of community for a long time. Christian community was created by God to be ever expanding with new believers. Fellowship to get deeper relationships will only spoil. What freshens it up and keeps it going is baby Christians that are excited about their new life, their new family, and their mentor or sponsor who is helping them through tough issues.

The bottom line: if you think your cell is stuck and becoming even more inward focused than before, prayer and planning are the keys to turning it around. Fast and pray, asking God to move mightily in your meetings and in the lives of the members so that they have a new hunger for the lost. Also, make some solid plans to move in their right direction with a Saturday strategic planning session. TOUCH has just released a good one if you want to use it in your cell group (*The Upward, Inward, Outward, Forward Workbook*).

Expanding the Cell

Expanding the Cell

A few weeks ago, I called a friend to see how he was doing. To my surprise, he said his cell was shrinking after a long dry season. This is a horrible feeling, mostly because cell leaders work hard and lay their lives down for their sheep. When the cell doesn't grow, discouragement can set in and take root.

Here are the four key areas to cell growth:

1. Upward
How is your personal prayer life? Do you pray with your spouse and family each day? Do you pray for your members every day? Do you devote a sizeable portion of every cell meeting to prayer? Your "vertical" relationship to Jesus is your lifeline. Don't let it wither! Make a plan with your cell to increase the different kinds of prayer mentioned in the next three months. Use a calendar!

2. Inward
How often do you connect with your members between meetings in face to face conversations? Do you spend lots of time hanging out or doing chores together? Growing cells have a strong intimacy between members that surpasses the cell meeting hours. This can be hard to do in urban areas, but it's vital to building a team of believers who can keep each other strong and move forward in purpose. Until it becomes second nature, use the

calendar mentioned in #1 and schedule times for personal interaction. Soon enough you'll be just like family and it will flow naturally.

3. Outward
Are you inviting lost people to come to your meetings? Have you thrown a party for everyone on your street yet? How about helping a cell member start a Bible study at the office? Evangelism is the key to excitement in your group! I have a new Christian in my cell group right now, and every week he fills the air with a crisp new understanding of Jesus and reminds me of what it was like so long ago. This is what cell life is supposed to be like all the time! Make plans now to involve the lost in your meetings and gatherings, and serve them to show them the love of Jesus in a tangible way.

4. Forward
Do you have interns or apprentices? Are you giving them ownership of the meetings, ministry visits, and other responsibilities? If you want to multiply your personal ministry and the vision of your church, you must raise up new leaders! Use that calendar to schedule "shadow" times when they will follow you to ministry visits, leadership meetings, and help them lead the cell, becoming a shepherd to your members. This way your group can multiply, or you can launch new groups and keep the number of people in the group manageable.

Question: NO ONE WANTS TO MULTIPLY

Help! My cell is exploding with new Christians and no one wants to multiply the group! What did I do wrong, and what should I do now?

Answer: The best way to prepare a group of people for any kind of change is to prepare them well in advance. The leader who asked this question didn't indicate whether the vision of the cell had been communicated regularly during the cell cycle. It's is in the best interest of the members and the new Christians present to describe a complete cell cycle — including the five stages of cell life-for each of the members individually in the beginning and as a group frequently throughout the days you are together. When the believers in your group begin to live out the understanding that your cell group is a platoon designed to share the Gospel and storm the gates of Hell to set captives free, multiplication will be an exciting time.

The best thing to do at this point is to share the vision and state the obvious. In your next meeting, discuss lines of communication. You'll want to help your cell members understand this key ingredient to productive interaction between members.

$$N \times N - N = CL$$

The number of people in your group, multiplied by the same number, minus the number equals the communication lines (i.e. 5 x 5 - 5 = 20 communication lines) Can you do the math and figure out how many communication lines you'd have if your group had 20 people in it? 380 lines of communication! That's a lot of talking and listening for each member to feel heard and understood!

The reality of communication lines may not hit your members right now. As they think back on huge cell meetings and the fact that at this size they can't get to know everyone well, they will feel the reality of the situation. Intimacy quickly leaves a group of this size. Without intimacy, transparency will be gone too, edification becomes rare, and your members will not feel pastored after a short time. Too many people in this recipe make failure for many.

Keep your group to no more than 15 or 16 people. As you grow near 12 members or 6 months, give the responsibilities of the meeting and most of the weekday activities to your interns. Then work on preparing hearts for multiplication, launching groups or starting a new thing called a G12. This is an innovative way to retain your cell members for life (no multiplication!) and help them all launch groups of their own on another night of the week. It makes an organizational chart messy, but it's quite effective for the kingdom, so ask your pastor to help you do this if you're interested.

uestion: STAGNATION IN THE CELL GROUP

My group has been together for over a year now. We haven't grown much, and I really think boredom has set in. We know each other's jokes, issues and struggles, and it's getting stale. What should I do?

nswer: You have a number of ways to correct your situation, but all of them will require the help of your pastor or the leadership above you. The options offered below *must* be done with the help and knowledge of your leadership. In fact, some of them won't be popular with your members, so it would be a lot easier on you (the cell leader) to get them to introduce the strategy and carry it out. After all, if someone has to be the "bad cop" in cell life, it shouldn't be you!

Regardless of what you choose to do, it's important to "state the obvious" in your next meeting:

a. Share the fact that the group has been together a long, long time and it isn't as dynamic and helpful in reaching the lost as it was in the beginning or at all.

b. Then, ask your members to share with the group if they agree or disagree. (What you want to do is build ownership for your current situation.)

c. Ask them what factors have contributed to a lack of growth in the group. Let them struggle with this!

d. If you sense a time of prayer and confession is needed for a lack of passion for the lost, open the group up to do this.

e. Make some plans with a "who will do what by when" accountability system for change. Plan an evangelistic cell meeting and invite the lost . . . design a "bring a friend" to the Sunday service for just your group and go out to eat afterward . . . get creative, but do *something* to connect to the lost and follow through on it.

f. Make sure your cell group knows that inward-focused groups die a slow death. If you're not reaching out and growing, it's not a cell group!

Now, here is the standard way cell church pastors remedy this problem:

Give the cell 90 days to turn it around with some new life or it must be disbanded. The pastoral leadership visits the group every other week or so during this time and is very pointed with the members that the group exists to serve others and grow with new Christians. He or she must help your group members see the hidden potential within for reaching friends and family for Jesus!

If this doesn't work, the group members are invited to join other groups that are effectively reaching the lost and growing. The original group is dissolved. You may think the cell leader would feel bad about this, but this is usually not the case. The leader wants the group to grow and is quite relieved that the burden has been lifted!

Or, the members will be added to a couple of newly multiplied groups. Typically, the stagnant group does not join another group as a whole. Part of the problem is usually that the group is a bad mix (evangelistic-wise, but probably not friendship-wise.)

This second option is a new idea from the G12 model, so hang on to your cell agenda! This will only work in certain situations where the members desire to evangelize, but don't want to populate their existing group for some reason (distance to weekly meetings, relationship issues, etc.)

Each member should be encouraged to start a weekly Bible study at the office or in their neighborhood as soon as possible. These Bible studies should be simple and only go for 8 to 10 weeks. The pastoral staff must supply the study. The Bible studies are held at another time during the week and the cell continues to meet as usual.

Each week, a complete update must be given on the status of each meeting, the names of each members, etc. Most of the time will be spent interceding for the Bible study participants.

When these participants come to Christ, the cell members will be coached to a) bring them to the cell meeting as new converts or b) plan to launch a cell and get trained as a cell leader as soon as possible. Group members can remain in the original cell as new leaders or be released to work with their own cell. That would be up to the leadership of your church.

It's a tough situation when groups don't grow and something must change. Most of the problem lies in the fact that the vision for the cell group hasn't been communicated enough or effectively. It could also be the case where the cell members just don't care about reaching the lost, or it's less important than other things.

My dad has this funny saying — "Keep the main thing the main thing." For a cell group, the main thing is reaching out. Let nothing get in the way of your primary directive and always run everything you do and plan to do through the "main thing" filter to make sure it's keeping you on track!

Question: AVERAGE LIFE-SPAN OF A CELL

I look at my cell, we haven't moved through the stages of cell life to multiplication. What's the average life of a cell group?

Answer: I could give the standard answer of 9 to 12 months as we have seen in America, but I don't think this would answer your question and get to the reason you asked it! Hopefully, this will help you understand why some cells have a life of 6 months and others have a life of 12 months or more.

Studies have shown that a small group of Christians who meet together weekly for more than a year become very lethargic in community building and outreach. They know each other's life stories, jokes, witty comebacks, and personal issues that they don't want to deal with, and they're too comfortable doing nothing to be any good in purpose-driven team thinking.

To be fair, I've seen some wonderful turnarounds in "old" cell groups, but most have to be reorganized into new groups and refocused on the purpose of the cell group. This problem is indicative of an upper and middle leadership issue and a cell leader level issue.

1. The senior pastor must communicate the vision of the cell groups from the pulpit in various ways on a weekly basis. Jesus said we're just like sheep, and He was right. Sheep forget to come in out of the rain, they forget where they are, and if the green grass and water isn't easy to see, they will starve to death. The vision to reach lost people for Jesus through the cell relationships must be recast often or the members and cell leaders alike will forget the primary purpose of the group. This can be done by

sharing the stated vision, sharing how the senior pastor is working with unbelievers himself in a cell environment, and inviting new Christians to share how they came to Christ through a cell. If the body is not regularly reminded that the focus of the cell is outreach, they will quickly turn the groups into spiritual "hot tubs" and just sit and soak.

If your pastor isn't casting the purpose of your cell group regularly, please don't get me in hot water with him by saying "Randall just emailed me and said you're doing a lousy job and you should start . . ." That, my friend, would not be fair to anyone! What you should do is to appeal to him that you feel your cell is losing their passion for the lost and you really need help. Ask him if he would share his own efforts to reach his friends for Jesus from the pulpit and allow leaders and members to give brief testimonies of the power of cells to reach the lost.

2. The pastoral staff and supervisors must hold the cells accountable for outreach and share about their efforts to reach the lost regularly, as the pastor must do. From your end as a cell leader, turn in your current *"oikos"* list of unbelievers for your cell to him or her. Give your supervisor or pastor permission to ask you about the relationship development that must occur to see them won for Christ (ask for strong accountability so you don't forget either!) Also ask him or her to help you determine who is ready for the challenge of leadership. Remember, these people are here to help you become and stay successful!

3. There are stages in a successful cell group, and to some degree, all cell groups go through these stages to get to outreach and see multiplication. They are as follows:

The Acquaintance Stage — We don't know each other well, so being honest is hard and we need more time together to really feel we can open up. You can help here by just being friendly and making sure everyone gets to spend time together outside of the meeting to really come to know the other people in your cell.

The Conflict Stage — We now know each other enough to open up and remove our masks, but we don't like what we see in others when we do. They remind us of a past hurt or person and we place our bitterness on them; we don't agree with the way they understand parts of the Bible; we don't like the way they raise their children; they are annoying and their personalities are abrasive; they are nice enough, but they constantly talk about their problems and won't deal with them and get past the issues. You can help by working through these issues and help your members to love one another with God's love, which looks through personality conflicts and unresolved issues at the child of God within. (Most Christians have never done this in church life . . . they just ignore the people or move churches. In cell life, you'll never grow until your members understand they must work through issues and move on to an abiding, Christ-centered love for one another.)

The Community Stage — The group has resolved issues and can now work as a team to reach the lost for Christ if they understand the complete vision for cells. Many cell members think "deep community" is the final goal of a cell group, and they are wrong. Making intimacy the goal of the cell is like trying to create heaven on earth while millions go to hell all around them. They must see community as the most powerful force on earth to storm the gates of hell to set captives free and use it as a weapon against Satan. Get the picture? Help your cell by telling them that community gets stale and boring if we don't harness the power of it to build the Kingdom. That is indeed why God gave it to us!

The Outreach Stage — The group is inviting numerous people to cell meetings, parties, and events to expose them to Christians and raise their awareness of a "personal, living relationship with Jesus Christ," not just church attendance or praying when you're really in a jam. This is the most fun part of cell life, and if you've never been here and seen it happen, you don't really understand what cell groups are all about. Get your members to work together as a team to win the lost and you will have the most fun you've ever had in your life!

The Multiplication Stage — The group has seen growth from outreach efforts, has raised up two new cell leaders who will work with the cell leader and intern in the next cycle. The group is large enough to have two small cells of 7-8 people in regular attendance after multiplication, and they've had to meet this way in different rooms of the same home for a couple of weeks to make good communication possible.

It will take 9-12 months to go through these stages in your first cell cycles as you learn about cell life; it decreases to 6-9 months when your cells are filled with new believers. The reason is that these new believers have been told from day one that the Bible says to reach out to friends, and they have never been long term "pew warmers." In addition, they are excited about a new life in Christ and naturally tell their friends. When this happens in your cell group, be sure to be on the prowl for emerging leaders or leadership potential in individuals. You will need it soon!

**uestion:** **PREPARING FOR MULTIPLICATION**

What practical things should a cell leader be doing in preparation of a cell multiplication?

nswer: As always, the first thing you should do is pray! Ask God to give you wisdom to approach each family in your group in a way that will make them feel valuable. Pray that they will understand the vision of your cell group (to stay small enough for intimacy, to train leaders, and to reach the lost as a team).

The next thing to do is to sit down with your intern(s) [by the time you need to multiply, you should have three: one who's acting as a co-leader at this point and two new ones who will begin as soon as you multiply your group] and pray more! When you meet, ask yourself and your interns this very important question:

"Has the intern taken ownership of the existing group and loved the members sacrificially to the point where they will follow him or her?"

If the answer is no, your multiplication may fail. You *must* give away the ownership of the cell to your intern(s) so they can earn the trust of the members who will go with them and to learn while under your supervision and guidance.

Then, meet with the pastor above you and/or your coach. They may know things about members (counseling matters that aren't discussed, but flagged as concerns) that will change your decision of who will go with whom when it's time to multiply. Your coach or pastor should also help you create two balanced groups, taking into consideration the following:

1. Number of children in each group and their ages (critical issue!)

2. Number of healthy, growing Christians to make up a solid core.

3. Number of hurting believers, "do-nothing" and "just along for the ride" believers.

4. Number of baby Christians and who is mentoring/discipling them through your equipping system.

With answers to these considerations, forge a plan and approach each family. Your coach or pastor may join you in the visit, which should be in the home of the family.

Offer the plan for the individual families as a suggested plan, giving them all your reasoning (children, leadership, existing mentoring relationships, strong people). Ask them to pray about the matter for a week and get God's answer rather than their personal feelings or input from other people. This won't be easy for them, especially if it's the first multiplication, but it's a stretching experience that will do them good.

TOPICS

Section 1: Leading the Meeting
Cell Agendas, 11
Bible Studies in the Cell, 13
Cell Member Involvement, 14
God's Movement, 15
Deviation from Cell Agenda, 16
Handling the Talker, 17
Disruptive Cell Members, 19
The Difficult Cell Member, 22

Section 2: Developing Leaders
Self-Study Equipping Track, 27
Groups of 12, 29
Age and Cell Leadership, 31
Time Management, 33
Lack of Commitment, 35
Leadership Qualities, 36
Leading the Opposite Sex, 37
Ministry to People of the Opposite Sex, 38
Accountability in the Cell, 39

Section 3: Entering into Community
Small Group vs Cell Group, 43
Becoming Family, 45
The Role of Prophesy, 47
Marketing Schemes, 48
Building New Relationships in the Group, 51
Healthy Cells, 53

Section 4: Reaching Out
My Cell is Not Growing, 59
Ideas for Outreach Events, 62
"Oikos" Evangelism, 66
Neighborhood Community, 68
No Desire for Evangelism, 70
Motivation for Evangelism, 71
Inward-Focused Warning Signs, 73

Section 5: Expanding the Cell
Key Areas to Cell Growth, 77
No One Wants to Multiply, 79
Stagnation in the Cell Group, 81
Average Life Span of a Cell, 84
Preparing for Multiplication, 88

CELL LEADER EQUIPPING RESOURCES

SHEPHERD'S GUIDEBOOK, *by Ralph W. Neighbour, Jr.*
This thoroughly tested book will equip your cell leaders for success and
train them to listen to God for their cell members, develop community
and lead people into relationship evangelism. Not only will your cell
leaders gain the tools for leading a cell meeting, they will also learn to
pastor their flock and multiply the ministry of your church. 256 pgs.

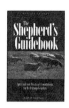

CELL LEADER INTERN GUIDEBOOK
Prepare your interns for cell group leadership before they begin their
ministry. This eight weeks of training will give interns confidence to
lead all the parts of the meeting, care for people through the stages of
cell life, and minister to the hurting. This book lays the foundation for
a long life of successful ministry. 144 pgs.

CELL LEADER INTERN TRAINER'S GUIDE
This user-friendly Facilitator's Guide, along with suggested reading
from *The Shepherd's Guidebook, The Cell Leader Intern
Guidebook* and *Ordering Your Private World* will prepare your cell
leader interns for fruitful ministry. This guide explains the
schedule and the content for the "Intern Weekend" and provides
the teaching outlines and transparency masters for the eight weeks
of intern equipping. Your church will have tested, equipped and
mentored cell leaders through the use of this proven system.
73 pgs. plus 76 overhead masters.

UPWARD, INWARD, OUTWARD, FORWARD WORKBOOK
Improving the 4 Dynamics of Your Cell Group, *by Jim Egli*
You can now take your cell leaders and interns through the same
strategic planning workshop TOUCH offers across the country!
    This easy to use workbook, combined with the facilitator's
presentation (a FREE download from our website) will help your cell
groups grow in the four basic dynamics of healthy cell life. Upward:
Deepening your relationship to the Father; Inward: Deepening
community between cell members; Outward: Reaching the lost for
Jesus successfully; Forward: Developing and releasing new leaders.
72 page student workbook

303 ICEBREAKERS:
At last ... 303 ways to really "BREAK THE ICE" in your cell group!
You will never need another icebreaker book. This collection places at
your fingertips easy-to-find ideas divided into nine categories, such as
"Including the Children," "When a Visitor Arrives" and "Lighthearted and
Fun." This is a needed reference for every cell meeting. We've included
instructions on how to lead this part of the meeting effectively. 156 pgs.

ADDITIONAL RESOURCES FROM TOUCH ON CELLS

WHERE DO WE GO FROM HERE?
THE 10TH ANNIVERSARY EDITION, *by Ralph W. Neighbour, Jr.*

With updated data on new cell church models, new information on equipping and harvest events and practical teaching on how to begin a transition, this book will continue to stir hearts to dream about what the church can be. You will find hope for the church in North America and discover the new things that Dr. Neighbour has learned over the last 10 years. Share this vision with a friend. 400 pgs.

THE SECOND REFORMATION, *by William A. Beckham*

Don't jump head-first into a cell church transition or church plant without reading this book! Beckham brilliantly walks you through the logic of a cell/celebration structure from a biblical and historical perspective. He provides you with a step-by-step strategy for launching your first cells. This wonderful companion to Neighbour's material will ground you in the values and vision necessary for a successful transition to cells. 253 pgs.

LIFE IN HIS BODY, *by David Finnell*

Communicate the vision of the cells to everyone in your church with this simple tool. The short chapters followed by discussion questions clearly define cell life for your leaders and members so that they can catch a lifestyle of prayer, community and evangelism. This book will give your church hope and vision as your members discover the possibilities of the New Testament community. 160 pgs.

CellGroup JOURNAL

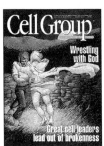

CellGroup Journal, unlike any other periodical, is focused on the needs and desires of cell leaders in your church. Every quarterly issue contains practical feature articles and columns from some of the most respected leaders in the US including Ralph W. Neighbour, Jr., Billy Hornsby on leadership, Karen Hurston on evangelism, Gerrit Gustafson on worship, Sam Scaggs on missions, and Larry Kreider with a closing note on a variety of topics. Pastor's get fed too . . . each issue contains an article for pastors by a pastor who has learned a good lesson in cell life and wants to share. Bulk discounts are available for larger subscriptions. Call today to subscribe for all your cell leaders and staff!

Order Toll-Free from TOUCH Outreach Ministries
1-800-735-5865 • Order Online: www.touchusa.org